Hoʻolaʻa

*I nā kumuhula, nā hoʻopaʻa, a me nā ʻōlapa o ka
wā kahiko a me nēia au e holo nei na lākou i
hoʻolaʻa i ko lākou ola i ke aʻo ikaika a koʻikoʻi i
nā hula, nā mele a me nā oli. A i nā poʻe a pau i
kuʻupau i ola ko hawaiʻi mau loina hula.
E ola mau a mau ka mana o ka hula.*

Dedication

To the teachers and dancers of the hula past
and present who have dedicated their lives to
the rigorous disciplines of this most beautiful
dance, its songs and chants. And to all those
who have labored to preserve Hawaiʻi's most
significant and honored tradition. May the spirit
of the hula live forever.

oli

The Book that Dances !!!

Shuffle the pages front to back and watch Nani dance! She begins with the "oli" (chant), and dances through the pages until "lawa" (enough), and her last move is "pau hana" (finished).

Enjoy

*H*ula, ...The ancient dance of the Hawaiian Islands. A dance that not only portrays the grace and beauty of movement, but on which exudes a powerful and dramatic story. A dance which can depict a gentle breeze, love, the harvesting of food...or of death, sadness and war.

A dance from the heart and soul...

The dance of life...

After almost two centuries of misunderstanding and suppression, the Hula has survived!!! In the last decade, Hula has become stronger and has gained its rightful place of respect in the arts. And respected the Hula shall be!; as many generation of Kumu Hula have fought desperately to keep their traditions alive; often ruthlessly forced to teach his or her haumāna at hidden, secret locations... But did so in order to bequeath the precious knowledge of their ancestors to all the future generations.

The Hula has survived... and shall live forever in the souls of those who have danced it, and in the hearts of those who have witnessed it!!!

It is the intention of this book to portray the beauty of the Hula with photographs, and to educate the reader of the many disciplines necessary to properly execute the Hula.

I hope Kumu Hula, Hula students, and interested spectators alike will find the pages within to be both enlightening and educational.

Ron Laes

To my mother...

For without your love and understanding,

I would not have been able to truly

appreciate the beauty of the Hula.

Discipline
Dedication
Respect

*T*hese are the three key fundamentals of teaching the Hula. Without either of these ideals, the Kumu Hula cannot successfully teach his or her skill, and the haumāna will never properly learn the dance. It is imperative the Kumu Hula receives as well as imposes these ideals from and upon each member of the hālau.

Kumu Hula is a position not to be taken lightly, nor is their knowledge to be taken for granted, as they endlessly labor to gain and hold the highly honored title of Kumu Hula.

The duties of the Kumu Hula do not end with teaching the dance, but continue with the lessons of ethics, traditions, and customs... as well as spiritual and religious mana'o.

The Kumu Hula is a dedicated individual whose dancers, and halau are a reflection of their thoughts, dreams, and inspirations.

A creator of skill and style, devoted to the perpetuation of the Hula...

This is the Kumu Hula...

'a'ā	lava
'ae	yes
ahi	fire
'ai ha'a	a vigorous Hula danced with bent knees
'aina	the land, earth
alaka'i	to lead; assistant to the kumu
ali'i	chief; of nobility
'a'ole	no
'auana	modern hula
'aumakua	a personal god
haku	the head, or open ended neck lei
hālau	a place where hula is taught
haumāna	a student; in training
hula	the dance; dancer; to dance the hula
hula honu	imitations of the sea turtle in dance
hula ho'onānā	hula performed solely for amusement
hula mānai	squatting dancer strikes time on the floor with a stick
hula pahua	a fast hula increasing to a frenzy
hula pele	a sacred dance for the goddess Pele
huli	to turn
huli'ākau	to turn right
huli hema	to turn left
ikaika	strength, power
i lalo	to move downward
'ili'ili	small stones held in dancers hand and worked to mark time
i luna	to move upwards

kāhea	to call out steps, verses, commands
kahiko	ancient hula
kai	the ocean
kāne	man, male
kapa	(tapa) fabric made from pounded bark
kapu	forbidden, sacred, not to interfere
keiki	a child, children
kuahu	an altar
kahuna	an expert; usually in a specific field
kuleana	responsibility
kumu	a teacher; master
kūpe'e	a bracelet or anklet
kupu kupu	ferns for lei making
lā	the sun
lani	the sky, heavens
lei	a neck ornament made from flowers, nuts, shells, feathers, etc.
maika'i	good; correct
maile	a fragrant plant used for special leis
makai	the ocean
mana'o	a thought or belief
mauka	inland; towards the mountains
mele	songs
pā'ū	a woman's skirt
pele	the volcano goddess; lava flow
pua	flowers; blossoms
ua	rain
'ūniki	graduation exercises for the hula
wahine	woman; female

7

Kaholo (vamp)	Step right, left, right, and tap left foot next to right. Repeat same to left.
Ka'o (sway)	Put weight on right foot, lift left hip. Repeat on left side.
Hela	Point right foot out front at 45 degree angle. Hip out to left side. Repeat same to left side.
'Uwehe	Lift right foot up and then down. Lift right hip then lift heels and open knees at the same time, pointing the knees to the front for wahine – out for kāne. Repeat left side.
Lele'uwehe	Step forward with right foot, putting body weight on right foot. Hela with left foot, and bring left foot back into place, and Uwehe. Repeat same to left side.
Lele	Step forward with right foot, putting body weight on right foot. Bring left foot next to right foot. Repeat same to left.
'Ami	Place two feet slightly apart. Push weight and hips to left and circle hips around to back and over to right side lifting on the ball of right foot and complete the circle to the front. This is the right Ami, done in counts of 2 or 4. To reverse, you must end on the same side you started on, and pushing hips slightly forward and over to right side, begin same movement on the right side.

ho‘omākaukau	to get ready
pā	to signal to begin the dance with motions, sounds, or beating
lawa	enough
i mua	forward, before
i hope	behind, after
i lalo	down, below
noho	sit
kū	stand
kāhea	to call, or announce
huli	to turn
hana hou	do it again
maika‘i	good, fine
‘ae	yes
‘a‘ole	no

Oli

Oli... a chant using prolonged phrases in one breath, often used before and/or during a dance.
Oli were (are) used for several different occasions, not always pertaining to dance.

- as prayers, asking for wisdom, safety, etc.
- to recite genealogies
- to ask for permission to enter hālaus, forests, heiau, etc.
- to grant permission
- to honor a person, place, or thing.

(The emotional qualities of the voice are of important significance during the oli!)

Kaholo

14

Hula Kuolo

(pā ipu)

Hula danced in a sitting position.
In this dance, the **ipu** (gourd drum)
is beaten, and the dancer chants.

Hula Ki'i

*A*ncient dance where the
dancer assumes stiff postures, imitating
images. This dance is rarely seen
today, however when performed,
is of much significance.

Hula Noho

*A*ny dance performed while in a sitting position. Often performed with instruments such as the **'ili'ili**.

'ili'ili

oeoe

'ohe hano ihu

kāla'au

pū'ili

'ūlili

pūniu

kā'eke'eke

'ulī'ulī

ipu

ipu heke

pahu

*L*iving on an island so far from land, the Hawaiians had to be very resourceful, relying on available materials and plant life with which to make their clothing. Throughout the years, Hula costumes have changed depending on available materials and imports.

The ti leaf skirt is extremely popular due to the great availability of the plant as well as the versatility of the skirt itself. It can be left whole which produces a shiny, brilliant, broad skirt; or it can be shredded to make a more subtle swaying skirt. It can be worn by itself or over other dress. The ti leaf skirt can also be made to produce unique sounds, accenting a particular dance.

The ti leaf skirt is also fairly easy to make. There are many different methods of attaching the leaves to the main cord, however this style was selected as it produces a most aesthetic belt line pattern.

Be careful!!!
Do not cut through into the leaf.

Each ti leaf must be deboned.

Leave left side of knot
long... this is the belt tie.

Back

Front

$\mathscr{P}$ossibly the most well known of all hula costumes is the grass skirt.

Most people associate the grass skirt with the auana (slow, swaying modern dance), however it lends itself nicely to kahiko (ancient dance) as well. When used in the auana, the skirt is usually worn long. In kahiko, it is shorter, and often accompanied with ti leaf or other embellishments. Its flexibility enhances and exaggerates the dancers movements.

The grass skirt is the most practical of all the natural skirts, as it will not wilt or rot, and can be stored indefinitely and is readily available for impromptu performances.

The grass skirt is also very easy to make. A main cord is stretched horizontally and the raffia, (or other durable, flexible fiber) is folded in half and laced around the main cord. Pull the knot tight and proceed with the next, sliding the knots together.

The length can be adjusted by trimming the bottom. The fullness of the dress is determined by the number of strands used in each knotted hank.

Back   Front

E ola ka ʻōlelo Hawaiʻi

"Let the hawaiian language live"

Kapeka *Maui*

Na ka poʻe o ko kākou ʻāina
na ka mana o ko kākou kai
e hoʻomau ai i ka hula

*"The people of our land...
the spirit of our ocean
will perpetuate the hula."*

Nohealani *Maui*

E lana mālie kou mau ʻale

"*Let the wave flow gently*"

Jade *Molokai*

E hō mai ka ua
ka ua makamae
e hoʻomaʻemaʻe kuahiwi
e hōʻihi ʻuhane

---

*"Let the rain fall,
the precious rain.
Cleanse our mountains
purify our souls."*

Lupe *Tonga/Hawaii*

ʻO makamakaʻole
kuʻu awāwa maluhia

"*Makamakaole,*
My peaceful valley."

Roxanne *Maui*

Hele ʻia ka ʻāina
ʻauʻau ʻia ke kai
a hula pū kāua
ʻoiai lilo kāua i ke aloha

"Together we walk the land,
swim the ocean, and dance the hula...
together we share our love."

Anela – Rubin *California/Maui*

No laka ke koko e kahe nei
i koʻu kino, koʻu ʻuhane
iaʻu e hula ana

*"It is lakas blood I feel
pouring through my veins, my soul
as I dance the hula."*

Mailelauliʻi *Mexico/California*

No ka moana ku‘u mele
no nā nalu au e hula ai

"*From the ocean comes my song...*
of the waves I dance my dance."

Angie *Maui*

He lei poina ʻole

"My unforgettable lei"

'elua moku
'elua pu'uwai
e hula pū ana

....

"Two islands

Two hearts

Dancing as one."

Angie – Vernay *Maui/Oahu*

lawa

Alaula Moloka'i

"Sunset over Moloka'i"

Anela *California/Maui*

Iawa

*M*ahalo nui loa

To all those who have helped me with their thoughts and knowledge.

To my daughter Jessica for her faith.

To Diana for her patience.

To Kī'ope Raymond & Punana Leo O Maui for the Hawaiian translations and aloha.

To Kumu Hula Mailelauli'i Mendez for her patience and instruction.

To Anela Gutierrez for her mana'o and her beautiful dance.

To Gayle Miyaguchi & Na Kani O Hula for her implements and aloha.

To Kaui Souza and Kelly Tuzzolino for the wonderful leis, haku and kūpe'e.

To Sunny Kaikala for her time and mana'o.

To Nani Cabatingan for all her technical support, dance, patience, and aloha.

To Vic Gendel and Dow Foster for their inspiration and ideas.

And last, but not least, to all the dancers who withstood wind, rain, and fire to make these photographs possible.

Aloha...

pau hana

A hui hou ...

"*Until we meet again...*"

Published by Goldsmiths Publishing
P.O. Box 1046
Puunene, Hawaii 96784

Mainland U.S.A.:
P.O. Box 10054
Bainbridge Island, WA 98110

Cover design by Doug Behrens Design • Honolulu
Layout and Photography by Ron Laes
Illustrations by Peter Durand

Printed in Hong Kong